T0194760

# Sexuality Empowerment

## Jewels of the Earth

Rose Mari Grigsby

**author**HOUSE®

*AuthorHouse™*
*1663 Liberty Drive*
*Bloomington, IN 47403*
*www.authorhouse.com*
*Phone: 833-262-8899*

*Published by AuthorHouse  08/17/2022*

*ISBN: 978-1-6655-5388-9 (sc)*
*ISBN: 978-1-6655-5387-2 (hc)*
*ISBN: 978-1-6655-5386-5 (e)*

*Library of Congress Control Number: 2022904046*

*Print information available on the last page.*

# Contents

# Jewels

So precious and dear
Are you to me
So powerful are you within
But often these powers
Are regarded as mere gifts
Of a female birth dormant,
To be looked at and admired
Never to be utilized
Read this book and let the words
Of these prose reinforce the
POWER WITHIN BY
FEELING YOU.

*We were molded from earth*
*Just as the gold and diamonds*
*We are all priceless jewels*

*We are in sync with all*
*God's creations,*
*We are the mothers of all*
*That has ever been.*
*Pain quickly causes us to*
*Forget our worth*
*AS TIME PASSES*
*Tears may fall but not for you. Oh no,*
*For the memories of the*
*Shattered pieces of life,*
*That is denied by us*
*All due to blinding faith.*

*Each prose in this book*
*Opens with a new experience*
*And ends with hope.*

*Each prose is a chapter in a life*
*A story within itself,*
*Maybe your life*
*Maybe your story.*

*Today as you read, LOOK, SEE,*
*FORGIVE, AND UNDERSTAND*
*That this life of events*
*Is not just yours.*
*THIS IS MY WORLD too*
*And so many others like us.*
*So LET ME IN to share*
*MY PEACE with you*
*One jewel to another.*
*Sit, read, and allow yourself*
*To touch, find, be, enjoy,*
*And may you be*
*Greatly blessed,*
*UNTIL NEXT TIME.*

# Acknowledgments

*I acknowledge the Holy Spirit that dwells within
me. God, my father, for blessing me with insight
into the hearts of my many sisters around the world,
for we are linked by the spirit of our maker.*

*My parents, my grandparents, my children,
and friends who have stood by me
through the windstorms of my life.*

*I acknowledge God as my center, my source,
my root, and Jesus Christ, as my Savior.*

# Preface
## Jewels of the Earth

Gold diamonds jewels of old
None more precious than you.

Not locked in rocks
But free to behold
The grandeur of all life
Precious are you
Jewels of the Earth
Mother of life when you give birth
Nourish the world when you let
Feed
From the well of your body
You nourish all seeds

*Jewels of the Earth*
*Cherished are you,*
*You deserve all the good you can*
*Hold on to.*

*What passes you by is not lost*
*So don't cry,*
*All will be blessed none is denied*
*For the love you have*
*Burning inside*
*For God, mate, child, it can't hide*

*Pain felt teaches you not to break*
*But bend*
*Father God, Mother Earth,*
*Holy Spirit within*
*Protects you from harm.*
*When you think you can't win*
*Will pick you up time and again*
*Will keep you safe until the end*

*So hold on, stay firm*
*Claim all your battles as won.*
*Jewels of the Earth*
*Through you, all man has come*
*Remember, to yourself be true*

*And that, I, Rose Mari,*
*Am feeling you.*

# Emeralds

Love, Honest, and True

Self-disclosure

To Other

From You

# Come In

I am not tall and slender
I am not young and tender

Only my heart is tender,
But guarded
By the seasons of knowledge

I am not fashionable and polished
I am not a scholar
By man's standards
But I know the word of my Lord

*I am not a trinket to be displayed*
*To play the games of the world*
*By looking the part*
*Of the in-crowd*

*But my gentle manner will appease*
*A storm of discontent*
*And calm the fury*
*Of disappointing lies*
*Told by worldly eyes*

*I am not one*
*Who leads by force*
*Or brute domination*

*I am not one*
*Who lays down and plays dead*
*In the face of injustice*

*My eyes are open*
*My mind is open*
*My heart is open*

*Won't you come in!*

# Feeling You

I feel your courage,
I feel your pain
I see your tears,
Forever in my mind.

I feel so helpless,
All this rain,
Will we ever see the sun again?
In the middle of the night,
I hear your cries,
They awaken me.

*I feel so helpless, all this rain.*
*Angel of mercy, shine*
*I feel so helpless, all this pain*
*Angel of mercy, please shine.*

*Warm us*
*With your inner peace,*
*Love and strength*
*To put it all together again.*
*Angel of mercy,*
*Heal these hearts and minds*
*Angel of mercy, please shine.*

# The Witch

Why is he acting such a Witch?
Why is his manner so unique?
In that, it's not him at all.

Why does he not speak?
As the man I knew, so strong,
Not weak and rude
And crudely awkward

Who is the Witch anyway?
Who has taken my first love away?
And molded him into
An identity so foreign to me

In denial of what was.

*The Witch within has broken free,*
*The closet door has flown open.*
*The Witch I see is really,*
*Who he always wanted to be*
*This Witch is now free.*
*Well, what does that do for me?*
*My first love, a Witch,*
*Unknowingly*
*Well, now the Witch is free.*

# Freeway

*Freeway, Freeway*
  *Free but not for me*
    *Taking everyone to get*
      *Done whatever needs to be*

*Freeway, Freeway*
  *Day and night escape to*
    *Parks and harbors*
      *Streets and shops*
        *No wonder you stay busy*
          *Some people never stop*

*Freeway, Freeway*
*One day, I'll hitch a ride*
*One day, I'll be free*
*From these invisible bars*
*That keeps me hidden inside.*

# *Tears*

*Tears in the shower*
*Hidden by the water*
*Blending with the wetness*
*Of my face*

*Tears down these cheeks*
*As I weep in silence*
*Hiding pain I have claimed*
*To be my own*

*Tears down this chin*
*Always hidden by a grin*
*This mask of false contentment*

*Tears on my inside*
*Felt as I hid under this sheet*
*As I struggle for sleep*
*To send me on a journey*
*Of escape*

*Take this mind, body, and soul*
*Give me peace*
*And set me free*
*From these chains*
*That bind me*

*Break me free to serve,*
*Love, and spread*
*The light of your word.*
*Wipe these tears,*
*Send your light,*
*I pray this every night*

*I wait for your word*
*To return fulfilled*

*You never fail these tears,*
*This veil,*
*Victory is at hand,*
*Freedom waits.*

# Fire Opal

## Passion, Physical

## Awareness

## Responding to

## What's Really You

# Ragamuffin

Remnants of broken spirits,
Broken dreams,
Pieces of all that could have been
But never was
Floating downstream

Ragamuffin,
Dusty tattered and torn,
Scarred, bruised, battered,
And used
Falling down a mountain of sorrow

*Ragamuffin,*
*Cut loose those strings of doubt,*
*Find your tomorrow break free,*
*Jump in, capture what is yours*

*Catch that wave, ride that tide,*
*There is no more time to hide*
*Life does have a prize for*
*Ragamuffins*

*Ragamuffins,*
*Like you, like me*
*We won't drift hopelessly*
*In a sea of defeat*
*We will hold on to the tree*
*We will look toward the rainbow*

*We have a Savior, a hero,*
*He died for you and for me*
*On that tree*
*He blessed us*
*With a rainbow*

*A dove and open gates*
*Ragamuffin, rise,*
*Lookup*
*And be free.*

# *Memories of My Last Love*

*And his heart will stop and sign,*
*Then say, "Oh, what good times*
*And fond memories have I of*
*My last love."*

*Her breast full like a dove,*
*Gently perched on a limb,*
*Patiently waiting to be embraced.*
*I recall her touch*
*Tracing my body inch by inch,*
*Her eyes attentively reacting*
*To my every breath, as*
*The two of us became one,*
*Our silhouette dancing*
*To the twinkle of the stars*
*Under a moonlit night*
*Inviting more love, more passion,*
*More fire, with*
*Every moment of intrigue.*

*Yes, I remember my last love.*
*These memories locked away;*
*Safe from alterations,*
*Deep in my heart*
*Embedded in my soul,*
*My last love,*
*This memory*
*I will forever hold.*

# Shattered

Take my heart
Take my soul
But not for silver or gold

Roses, lilies, daisies of old
Fields, forests, and lakes
Moss growing on the roadside

Under the tree, you laid me down
My body adored so trustingly
Reviled me to the open sky
You did not try to hide

*The promise you made*
*To the girl in the shade*
*To love and forever hold dear*
*Broke this heart*
*When all fell apart*
*With the true meaning*
*You never made clear*

*You took this heart*
*You took this soul*
*You give not silver*
*You gave not gold*

*But a shattering lie*
*That will never die*
*Until the broken begins to heal.*

# No!
# Not for You

No! My body won't cry out
For you
Because it was not meant to be
But in my heart
You will always be
A pleasant memory

*No! I won't call your name*
*In the still of the night*
*Or long to hold you oh so tight*
*Because the night*
*Belongs to me only*
*With lonely whispers of love gone*

*No! I can't touch or hold or kiss*
*Or even afford to miss*
*Those sweet lips*
*I used to kiss, so lovingly*
*And tenderly*
*Every part of you melted*
*Into every part of me*
*Continuously*
*Loving me, loving you, but*
*No! my body won't cry out for you*
*Because you are gone yes,*
*Very gone in reality*

*Only in my heart and dreams*
*Will you ever be,*
*You are gone*
*Long gone*
*And forever*
*Gone*

# One Heart

*Fear*
*Where does it come from?*
*Where does it go?*
*Afraid of what?*
*Tomorrow?*
*Trying to go back? Where?*
*To yesterday?*

*To the time of safety and calm*
*In your arms*
*The time of trust*
*And holding on*
*Knowing you won't let me go*

*Maybe that's why I love you so*
*I'll never let go of yesterday*
*Or*

*Of the memory of that time*
*Of safety and calm*
*In your arms*
*As I meditate to stay strong*
*And go forward to*
*What life has in store for me*
*For us, together or apart*
*Two bodies*
*But one heart.*

# Two Hearts Afloat

*Two seasoned hearts*
*Afloat at sea,*
*Joined by the hip*
*For half a century*
*As time passes,*
*The love still lingers*
*Holding on to traditional vintage*
*But flirtatious youth teased*
*And taunted*
*The more adventurous of the two,*
*Saying, come run with us,*
*She's too slow for you*

*The love in the heart*
*Had never stopped flowing*
*But the offer to play, well,*
*The interest kept growing*
*'Til one day, it was thought*
*Who would notice if I jumped in*
*And played in forbidden seas,*
*A time or two,*
*Maybe three*

*I must satisfy this urge*
*To give it one last try*
*Before my motor gives out*
*Before my time to die*
*But how can I move as one*
*When there have always been two?*
*The mother ship has always been*
*What I've been used to*
*And to change my diet*
*To strange fruit*
*Could kill a fish like me,*
*Who's forgotten to swim*
*In hot water*
*Moves a little slow*
*And ducks too late*

*Two seasoned hearts*
*Afloat at sea*
*Joined by the hip*
*For half a century*
*The battle continues*
*'Til death do them part*
*The love will still linger*
*No matter how hard*
*No matter how tough*
*The going gets,*
*Each round makes for a more*
*Seasoned Vet*

*In sticking it out through*
*Thick and thin*
*And giving a kick to the head*
*Or the chin,*
*To the unfaithful bearer*
*Of shame and deceit*
*Remembered that*
*The father on high, one day,*
*They will both meet*
*With grace and forgiveness*
*They will take a seat*
*In the hall of fame with the saints,*
*Who hung in and stayed firm*
*From beginning to end*

*God's love endures forever,*
*So what can man do?*
*To tarnish the gift he has waiting*
*For you*
*Your reward it, not earthly*
*So what can man do?*
*To steal the victory*
*God has for you.*

# So I Wait

*In my distress, I seek serenity*
*But do not find it*

*In my distress I seek, I seek, and*
*Nothing is of comfort to me*
*For very long*

*In my distress, I ask*
*For a shoulder, a hand, a sign*
*Of some sort, to show*
*That I am not alone*

*In my distress,*
*My lonely anguish of existing*
*While in search of inner peace*
*The purpose, the reason for me,*
*The map I must travel to be free,*
*To leave this frame of mind*
*My spirit seeks its maker,*
*My body seeks its likeness*

*In no man have I found rest*
*Or an answer to end my quest*
*Of longing for the warmth*
*Of the nest that eagles fly to*
*High in the sky*

*The quest for the peace*
*Of the flowers in spring,*
*The warm glow of the sun gently*
*Caressing my face, and*

*The winds, sweet, flow*
*Against my entire being*
*Bringing with it the fragrance*
*Of spring, summer, fall,*
*Or even winter for they all know*
*Their purpose here but me,*
*Not a clue as to what I am to do*

*This is my distress*
*For I cannot elude to a safe place*

*I listen but do not hear*
*A voice to guide me*
*I cry out, but only*
*My echo returns*

*Perhaps, I'm in the wrong place,*
*The wrong time*
*Perhaps, I must wait*
*Until redeemed by my maker*
*Through a secret plan,*
*So I wait.*

# Amethyst

## Clarify Thoughts

## Touching the

## True You

# Your Chapter, My Verse

*I remember many times*
*When you were rude to me*
*Viciously unkind,*
*Then you'd say you loved me*

*I remember guilt and pain*
*That I just couldn't explain*
*In my heart or mind*
*It seemed a part of what it took*
*To be a chapter in your book*
*Yes, I was hooked and satisfied*
*To be a verse set aside*
*That you used to keep people out*
*Who gives you love and life*
*So freely*
*And you never give back*

*I blindly followed*
*Your dead-end lead*
*Until my heart started to bleed*
*With tears compiled of*
*Misplaced verses*
*Until I could no longer read*
*And I couldn't get free*
*I was too close*
*To close this chapter of misery*

*A cracked cup is never the same*
*A broken heart*
*Can it be mended again,*
*And again,*
*And again*
*From the same pain?*

*Dear Father above,*
*Give me the strength*
*To circumvent this madness*
*That I have played a major role,*
*I want out of this casting*

*Please give me courage*
*And confidence to trust in you*
*To send me forward in your love*
*With the light that is within me*
*Thank you,*
*For loving me*
*And showing me*
*How to be free.*

# *D*issing

*No need to diss your sister*
*Because of hostile ground*
*In times of stress,*
*You have at best,*
*A mutual tie that bonds*

*No need to diss your brother*
*Or really any other*
*In time of need,*
*You must adhere*
*To the common cause,*
*Survival*

*No need to diss yourself,*
*When times seem bleak and grim*
*There is a light*
*That shines so bright*
*And covers all the pain*

*The warmth you need*
*Is there inside,*
*Every heart has the seed,*
*It's planted deep within your soul,*
*Let the light in,*
*Let it grow.*

# Looking for Me

*I'm looking for me*
*In me*
*Deep down inside of me*
*To find me*
*But I only saw you!*

*Then, I asked me,*
*What could I do to find the me*
*That had turned into you?*

*You said there's really no me,*
*So why bother?*
*You've swallowed Me up in you,*
*To get out*
*Would take a long hard fight,*
*A struggle, a labor of love,*
*Of Me loving Me,*
*Instead of only you,*
*I know that is true*
*So now, what do I do?*

*To stop loving you so much*
*That I shrank, to a small voice*
*In a corner*
*Saying please set Me free*
*Let Me be Me*
*To find and love myself,*
*Yes, I want to love me.*

# Loving in Truth

*I never knew what I could do*
*To touch you from afar*

*I never thought*
*The things I bought*
*Would be forgotten relics,*
*Of love misplaced*
*From a heart untaught*
*To look for love in truth,*
*The love in truth I never knew*
*Even though*
*I saw right through you,*
*Your heart was shielded*
*By a patch,*
*You thought would heal you*

*Love in truth was out of sight*
*And I think you knew it*
*The light of day will send a ray*
*Of power to heal it*
*Then seal it*

*Just move the patch*
*And trust the light*
*Let love in truth prove it.*

# *Today*

*Today, I felt the wind*
*Against my face*
*I smelled the air, its freshness*
*Had been erased from my memory*

*The sunlight, warm and bright,*
*Hurt my eyes, a pleasant pain,*
*I squinted it away, then smiled*

*Could it be over, the storm,*
*The rain, the real pain of my life,*
*Or just the light*
*At the end of the dark?*
*Another turn in the maze of life,*
*This life has given without request,*
*This life! Am I really doing*
*My best?*

*Father, help me*
*To be free*
*Embrace my spirit,*
*Transform my heart,*
*Then stay with me.*

# As Time Passes

*You feel good, I feel nothing*
*You look good, I see nothing*
*Your words*
*Are so exciting and inspiring*
*You tell me, go on,*
*Don't give up*

*I'm numb, and blind, and lifeless*
*My breath has been taken away*
*My purpose evaded and detoured*
*My knees buckle*
*From time to time*
*As I stumble to fall, I look behind*
*You are there, not just air*

*My movements are unsure now*
*Because of past bruises*
*And bumps*
*See me, see me, I don't see me,*
*I'm blind*
*My head full of blank doubts*
*What is all this?*
*About life or death*
*Where is life?*
*After all, has been taken away*
*Where is the light?*
*Where is the glory?*
*I am but salt*
*Waiting to flavor*

*The sweet words of your truth,*
*Where is my youth?*
*Gone,*
*Taken by the world*
*But, ah, there still is time,*
*Use me, use me now,*
*For tomorrow may be too late*
*Tomorrow may never come*
*As we know it today,*
*Tomorrow is not promised*
*But every promise*
*Will be fulfilled.*

# This Is My World

*Strange people are all I see*
*In the closet,*
*On the street,*
*And this is my world?*

*Heroin, cocaine,*
*Poison in the vein*
*Coming to the surface*
*To stain the body and the brain*
*And this is my world?*

*Touch me not,*
*I have no feeling*
*I know not how*
*This all came about*
*But for now,*
*This is my world,*

*4 AM count, 8 PM count,*
*On line, in line,*
*Everything is count*
*And on Tine*
*And this is my world?*

*Time for crime, no, no, no,*
*Not all the time*
*Time for being born*
*Time for being black*
*Time for being brown*
*Time for being white*
*With no money around*
*And this,*
*This,*
*This is my world!*

# Sapphire

## Overcoming

## Sadness

## New Beginnings

# Music Man

He quietly seduced me
Into his bed
With the music from his heart
That came out of his head
Notes from his minuet
Melted like candles
In the still of the darkest night
Evaporating
Into the valley of deceit
Oh, but still how sweet it was
For a moment
It seemed like eternity
Filled with never-ending ecstasy

*He led me on a journey*
*Deep into his soul*
*Then challenged me to grab hold*
*For the ride of a lifetime*
*Then when my heart was unaware*
*He slipped away*
*Like the smoke into the air*
*As though as he was never there*
*The music faded*
*My heart still burns.*

# The Power Within

*A great windstorm arose*
*And beat my vessel so*
*That it weakened to the point*
*Of near destruction.*

*As the Holy Spirit slept*
*Within my soul,*
*Waiting to be summoned*
*By my will.*

*I cried out,*
*"Do you not care if we perish?"*

*A reply came, "Do you not care?"*
*Where is your faith?*
*Call on your power?*

*It's here within,*
*Rebuke the storm*
*And praise the Father,*
*Rise up in your faith,*
*Your power is within*
*Victory is in your hand.*

# *D*enial

As though we never were,
We pass, seeing
And not seeing
Knowing
But not wanting
To pull up the knowledge
Of our past

Not wanting the infection
Of the sores left unattended
To seep into now

This now
That will only last for now

*The pain of the past,*
*We never played out or resolved*
*Will just be there,*
*Increasing in intensity,*
*As we decrease in reality,*
*Until the major surgery*

*From a sore to a tumor,*
*To a cancer,*
*Filled with every angry thought*
*Unspoken*
*Every pain unacknowledged*
*To the point of death*

*You do kill me, yes,*
*Softly, slowly,*
*You kill me with denial*
*That anything is wrong*
*Or that nothing was ever right,*

*I must not die*
*Bring on the knife,*
*Let the surgery begin.*

# This Title

This title around my neck
A love affair has gone sour

The more I strive, the
Heavier the load of my labor gets

The web of duties given to me
Performed once so lovingly
Have burdened my mind,
Body, and soul
Now, it's love turned to hate
And I don't know how to escape

*I've worked my lifetime to*
*Stay afloat*
*But now, I want to jump*
*Off this boat*

*Look at that bird sitting in his*
*Nest*
*He does not labor, nor does he sow,*
*He eats, sleeps, flies, and rests*

*Who provides him this luxury?*
*Must I put in petition for him*
*To help me?*

*His yoke is easy, so I have read*
*He calls all who labor to rest*
*In him, could it be, that he*
*Will make a way for me?*

*He will*
*It is written.*

# *May I Love You*

May I love you?
For you are one of few,
Who my spirit gravitates to
May I love you?
Along with the many others,
You have mothered in your lifetime
May I join your spirit?
In laughter and pain, victories
Temporary setbacks
That tried to stain your courage

A pretty picture in your mind
That someone else has painted
A dream that lasted
A lifetime,
Now you are awake
And I see your heart
Quietly reaching out
So I ask with much respect,
Of the time and knowledge
Dreams and nightmares,
Your sleeping spirit has known
And now awakened,
To find me here
Asking you, my dear,
With withered lines of knowledge
On your face
Lines of time and trails
That will never be erased

*May I love you?*
*With the love of God's light,*
*The love that might comfort,*
*The fright*
*Felt by awakening to find*
*The dream you dreamed*
*Was not yours*
*But someone else's, all the time*
*A sleeping beauty*
*Blind then awakened*
*To find a lifetime*
*Gone by.*

# Pearls

Forgiveness

Smoothing over the

Hurt

Healing

# Forgiveness, Now, I Understand

*Through the rainstorm of tears,*
*Lasting through the years,*
*I understand now*
*That you were just a man*
*And none of my pain*
*Was part of your plan*

*I forgive you,*
*I understand now*
*That you were just a man,*
*Not perfect as I had pictured*
*But just another dapper dan*
*You didn't know how*
*To do anything*
*Other than what you did,*
*My pain*
*Was just an impersonal*
*By-product of your production,*
*Your master plan*

*Now, finally,*
*I forgive and release you*
*And I want you to forgive*
*And release me*
*Finally, I understand*
*The love burning deeply*
*Embedded in my soul*
*I will feel it eternally*

*I thank you for that love*
*And for the experience*
*Of being able to let it go*
*To develop and grow*
*In wisdom*

*For it has allowed me to grow,*
*To know that*
*The only perfect passion,*
*The only perfect love,*
*The only enduring love,*
*Is that love that comes*
*From God Almighty.*
*Above.*

# Intrigue

I've never looked at this before
At appears quite amazing
From this angle of calm
And patience,
As I sit to rest from stress,
I've never looked at this
From a relaxed view

This pattern richly endowed,
Amazing what I've overlooked
From day to day
Where have I been
All these years?

*Amazing what you see,*
*If you just take time to look,*
*It's hard for me to believe*
*That my kitchen floor*
*Has intrigued me.*

# My Peace

I send you my peace
I send past times
Of happy me and happy you,
I send, I send you,
A little piece of me

For me to be there right now,
Cannot be, so
I send you my peace

*Your future might seem bleak now,*
*But close your eyes*
*Daydream of what was*
*Let yesterday take you through*
*Today*
*And into tomorrow,*

*I do only what I can do*
*And that is*
*To send you my peace*
*A beat from my heart*
*A breath from my body*
*And words from my soul.*

# Let Me In

Sent by my Father
To enter, in this world of sadness
This world of sin
To do my part to bring an end
To suffering within

But this spirit can't find a home
A place to grow for a very long

*So much despair within these*
*Vessels*
*They push me out, they cannot feel,*
*They know not where my journey*
*Began*
*I know not where it ends*

*I can't find a place to enter in*
*Please stop one moment*
*To help a friend*
*Who's here again? Please, let me in*

*This one more birth might put an*
*End*
*Might save a soul, might lead it*
*Home*
*Give me a chance*
*To sprout and bloom,*
*A chance to end my brothers'*
*Gloom*
*A chance to do my Father's work*

*Please let me in, I can't desert*
*The task I have been given*
*From God's light to daylight*
*God's love to you.*

# *L*ife

Come dance with me, or
I will pass you by

Come dance with me, now
For I have no time to wait

Dance with me, quickly
Others want to drink of me
And be full

Dance with me, hurry
You have only one chance
Grab me before I pass you by

*Come dance,*
*My music is bittersweet, yes,*
*But the sweet seasons the bitter*
*To a blend of perfection*

*Dance, the band plays on,*
*The tune is never-ending*

*Take this dance, this chance,*
*Come! Dance,*
*The dance of life.*

# Diamond

Abundance

Prosperity

Total Body Purifying

Magnifying

# *Misread*

*I am sorry, I misread you*
*I took every negativity*
*As though it were aimed at me,*
*I did not realize*
*We were not meant to be*

*I misread everything*
*That came from your head*
*I aimed it at my heart*
*Like it was a target*
*Set to fall apart*

*I suppose,*
*I took this whole encounter*
*Too seriously*
*Instead of letting it be,*
*Whatever it was to be*

*I'm sorry, I misread you*
*And caused me pain.*

# Until Next Time

*I remember you entering me*
*And tears flowing freely*
*Down my face*
*The tears were tears of grief*
*And mourning*
*For I knew our time had ended*
*I knew that this entry*
*Would be the last*
*For you and me*
*Our time had passed*

*We did all we could do*
*We loved*
*We laughed*
*We cried*
*We tried it all and now*
*The end*

*All things have a beginning*
*And all things have an end*
*And all that is in between*
*Is time, precious time*
*Happy and sad*
*Never to be relived*
*Except in our hearts, our minds*
*Until the next time,*
*We fall in love.*

# These Arms

These arms of mine
Are empty now
But it's okay

For there was a time
When they were filled with you
Through and through
You filled me up
With you

*These arms of mine extended*
*Reaching for the memory*
*Of your warmth*
*Securely wrapped in my bosom*

*These arms, these arms*
*Now empty*
*How can this be*
*When you said*
*You belonged to me*

*But, just like a bird*
*You longed to be set free*
*So I let you go now*
*These arms*
*Empty.*

# Look, See

Look see! What is in me
See the love and beauty
You once held captive
Look see!
Like a butterfly in a cocoon
Sleeping
Waiting to be freed
To spread the beauty
Found within me
This love
Trapped by you

*Look, see, the new me*
*Free from pain*
*Free from chains*
*Linked to your heart*
*You tried to kill*

*This will of mine*
*Given to me*
*In the beginning of time*

*My spirit is still filled*
*With the love*
*You could not control*

*You could not hold these wings*
*My pride, I will not hide*
*See me*
*Strong now*

*I refuse to die*
*I release all hurt*
*Now, watch me*
*As I fly.*

*Stress-free and loving past experiences from a distance. Some of them hurt but look at your wings, stronger now, flying confidently.*

_____

_____

_____

_____

_____

_____

_____

_____

_____

_____

_____

_____

_____

_____

_____

_____

_____

_____

_____

_____

*So where are you going? What now? Talk to yourself.*
*Answer the questions!*

_____

_____

_____

_____

_____

_____

_____

_____

_____

_____

_____

_____

_____

_____

_____

_____

_____

_____

_____

*Ask for guidance. It will come. Fear and hesitation are not an option.*

*PATIENCE! Be anxious for nothing. True love will love you back. BE PATIENT!*

_____

_____

_____

_____

_____

_____

_____

_____

_____

_____

_____

_____

_____

_____

_____

_____

_____

_____

*What on the inside, what's on the outside, what's in the middle, you are in the center of it all. Just relax and think. You are the director of your life.*

_____

_____

_____

_____

_____

_____

_____

_____

_____

_____

_____

_____

_____

_____

_____

_____

_____

_____

*You are unique, the only one ever made. Know that! Own that! Be your own you! Kiss yourself! Love yourself!*

_____

_____

_____

_____

_____

_____

_____

_____

_____

_____

_____

_____

_____

_____

_____

_____

_____

_____

_____

*Open arms you give, and open arms you receive. Never be too full. Fear not, always be open to applying agape love, (God's Love). Having a loving attitude will get you through.*

_____

_____

_____

_____

_____

_____

_____

_____

_____

_____

_____

_____

_____

_____

_____

_____

_____

_____

*No disappointments, life is ever-changing. What's your next change?*

_____

_____

_____

_____

_____

_____

_____

_____

_____

_____

_____

_____

_____

_____

_____

_____

_____

_____

_____

*Go with the flow, or be still, and know that you are forever loved by your maker, and no matter what your physical appearance, you were made in his image, perfect. In his eyes perfect.*

_____

_____

_____

_____

_____

_____

_____

_____

_____

_____

_____

_____

_____

_____

_____

_____

_____

*What are you vibrating today? The good, the bad, and the ugly, like a boomerang, will always come back.*

_____
_____
_____
_____
_____
_____
_____
_____
_____
_____
_____
_____
_____
_____
_____
_____
_____
_____

*Work, work, work, and WORK again, for what, what, WHAT. Remember your maker's gift to you, the Sabbath, rest and enjoy.*

_____

_____

_____

_____

_____

_____

_____

_____

_____

_____

_____

_____

_____

_____

_____

_____

_____

*Look at yourself in the mirror and ask, "Who am I?"*

_____

_____

_____

_____

_____

_____

_____

_____

_____

_____

_____

_____

_____

_____

_____

_____

_____

_____

_____

_____

*Look at the new you, describe this new you.*

_____

_____

_____

_____

_____

_____

_____

_____

_____

_____

_____

_____

_____

_____

_____

_____

_____

_____

_____

*Question: Where is the old you?*
*Answer: Evaporated into experiences, growth, and lessons.*

_____

_____

_____

_____

_____

_____

_____

_____

_____

_____

_____

_____

_____

_____

_____

_____

_____

*What lessons? It's okay. Spit it out. Acknowledgment
is good for the soul.*

_____

_____

_____

_____

_____

_____

_____

_____

_____

_____

_____

_____

_____

_____

_____

_____

_____

_____

*Impose on yourself. Put it out there.*

*See it, believe it, but don't relive it, grow from it.*

_____
_____
_____
_____
_____
_____
_____
_____
_____
_____
_____
_____
_____
_____
_____
_____
_____
_____

*WHAT IS IT? Write it down, remember, everybody has an IT, WHAT IS YOUR IT?*

_____

_____

_____

_____

_____

_____

_____

_____

_____

_____

_____

_____

_____

_____

_____

_____

_____

_____

*Welcome in the NEW you, feel the NEW you, kiss the NEW you, love the NEW you.*

_____

_____

_____

_____

_____

_____

_____

_____

_____

_____

_____

_____

_____

_____

_____

_____

_____

*No denial, no anger, no blame, no guilt, no depression, no pain, no fear, no loneliness, no self-imposed isolation, just know that you are loved. Love conquers all, so demonstrate self-love, and more love will come to you. Keep loving. Never stop loving! Every living thing has a divine purpose and our purpose is to love with the love of our maker starting with his greatest creation—YOU. Yes, you are a catalyst. You radiate.*

_____

_____

_____

_____

_____

_____

_____

_____

_____

_____

_____

_____

_____

_____

# Special Thanks and Much Love

*For feeling me, touching me.*
*Holding my hand, and not letting go:*
*Anita and Brigadier General*
*Celes King III*
*Karen Zaleski-Roach*
*Ivery Walters*
*Marcia Sharice Massey*
*Jeannie and Fred Rothfuss*
*Kimette and Chad Hughes*
*Mrs. Michaelann Dievendorf*
*Clifton Anthony Hinds*

Printed in the United States
by Baker & Taylor Publisher Services